BACK

FROM

DEAD

No Nonsense Business Turnarounds

By

Saurabh Maheshwari

Ram Parthasarathy

Dedications-

My Parents and My wife who have been my pillar of strength through-out my life. They have given me the freedom to take my decisions, make my mistakes and yet have remained the rock on whose foundations I have built my life. Thank You Papa. Thank You Mummy. Thank you Megha. Also dedicated to my son Dev who has shown me the value of adaptability, resilience, patience and staying happy in all situations (he is a very active child but has not stepped out of the house for the last 40 days).

Saurabh Maheshwari

All those people, remembered and forgotten, who have been part of the long road of learning for me, and without whom this book would not have been possible!

Ram Parthasarathy

Table of Contents

Introduction

At the time of writing this book, COVID -19 has spread across the world and continues to ravage world economies. There are complete or partial lockdowns implemented in 90% countries of the world bringing the world economy to a grinding halt. Government after Government is announcing large rescue and stimulus packages. The world economy is in a state of shock. The news flows across financial channels have the following theme –

- *Stock markets across the world are down 20%-50% from peaks, signaling various degrees of recession*
- *All Businesses have come to a standstill.*
- *Joblessness in major economies across the world is at the highest.*
- *Whoever still has a job is facing varied degrees of salary cuts.*
- *Governments across the world have launched trillion-dollar rescue packages.*
- *Airlines are closing down for good every week.*
- *Start-ups are expected to be battered and a lot of them will die very shortly.*
- *Businessmen are wondering when will the businesses and cash flows start again,*
- *Restaurant, Hotels, Malls, Movie Theatres are affected even more.*
- *By varied estimates, 30%-50% of businesses are expected to shut down.*

You, as owner of a business, are one of the most affected people. Your entire life revolves around the business that you have nurtured over a period of time. All your employees look up to you for guidance and support. Your vendors expect payments and the government expects that you will continue producing and continue paying taxes.

You do not have the safety of a pension and normally all your money is tied up to your enterprise.

With all this going on (and for most of the business owners, even before COVID 19), most businesses are in trouble. Trouble typified by Lack of Cash flows and Funds, Continued Losses, Increasing Indebtedness, Supply Chain disruptions due to lack of funds, inability to invest in equipment's or manpower, and the sleepless nights that you have.

So, the next question is what is ailing your business? And what will you do to change that? How will you turn it around and become the superstar of business who everyone looks up to?

This book intends to tell you what you can do to turn around your business. This book intends to break up the turnaround into its individual issues and what can you do to change that. The Book is essentially divided into 3 sections -

Section I – Real Life Examples – Real life turnaround examples with a variety of basic underlying problems from the author(s) personal experience. These will give you a small glimpse of how we as professionals have tackled different situations and different problems. This will be a good start to assessing the problems you may face as a business and also if you are lucky, you will one of the case studies will mirror your problems.

Section II – Framework to correctly assess and identify your problems – This is where we will give you quick tools to correctly identify and assess the problems that your businesses are facing.

Though you can do this assessment yourself, but we will very strongly suggest that you get this assessment done either from an outside consultant or from someone who is not involved in your business. We would suggest that you do not do it yourself personally as there a lot of bias which creeps in when we try and assess our own business. Even your Financial Advisor, Banker, or a close friend will normally do a better job of this. The next job after assessment is to rank the issues in terms of gravity so that we can prioritize working on solving them.

Once you identify the particular situation, you will have the choice to go straight to that part in the book for very concise tips and solutions. However, we strongly suggest that you go through the entire book for other ideas and thoughts which will surely ignite the way you think about your business.

Section III – Action points for Turning Around the Business – This is the key part of the book wherein we will divide the issues identified earlier into categories and then will try and give our take on how the same should be solved. This will be more of a suggestion mode to ignite your thinking and you may find that yourself doing more than one thing at a time.

What this book is not about

This book is not filled with jargons and high-level concepts which may or may not be of use. This book is also certainly not a magic pill which will make your business a profit and money generating machine overnight. But this book will certainly help you to identify what ails your Business and what can be the possible solution to the problems that you are facing. Using the concepts given here, you can put your house in order and make your business profitable the way it should be.

However, before taking any action basis the content of this book, we would advise you to consult with you Accountant, Legal and Financial Advisors and also run it through your family members and people you trust.

Let's start.

Saurabh Maheshwari

Ram Parthasarathy

May 2020

PART I: Real Life Examples

Companies can become distressed due to a variety of reasons. However, in most cases the reasons are fairly obvious, and the common thread running through all of these situations is that there has been a lack of initiative to tackle problems which are clear and visible, due to what We like to call "Blind Management Syndrome". Very rarely, a company may become sick due to circumstances completely outside its control, for example during the current COVID crisis. Even in such situations, a number of things can be done to alleviate the pain.

And, how can anyone write a book on turnarounds without Examples. And ideally, these should be from real life and from personal experience. What we have here are 6 Examples which fulfill both the criteria – they are very much real and we have been a part of them. The names, locations and businesses may have been changed a little, but these are as real as they get.

Example One: Pharmaceutical Industry

Operations in a price control regime, focus needs to be on process efficiency

A pharmaceutical major was manufacturing large volume parenteral drugs (injectables, also called IV). Due to regulation of the price by Government, there was no possibility of increasing the price of the product. The volumes were more or less guaranteed as the market was ready to take whatever we produced including any increases in production if we can manage that. With costs rising year on year, margins were being steadily eroded and the owners wanted to check that and get the margins back up.

What did we do:

Desired outcome: Clearly, the need was to ramp up volumes without increasing overhead costs, so that the gross profit and hence net profit would improve.

To do that, the following steps were taken:

1. The process was re-visited, and one unnecessary step of solution preparation was eliminated. The company had two steps of solution preparation and solution mixing. These were combined into one. The result was savings in labor and savings in power costs, as well as reduction of the overall time taken by the process.

2. Introduction and implementation of best in class predictive maintenance techniques for all critical equipment, to ensure that machine up time was 99% plus. This improved from about 75% uptime earlier to close to 95% in a very short time. This really help us in ramping up volumes without any further investments.

3. That's all we did. No extra labor, no extra overhead. In fact, overheads declined due to process reduction.

So, what were the results of all the actions that we took?

Take a look at the comparison below: (Sales are in million units)

	Before			After	
	Qty	Value		Qty	Value
Sales	45	450		60	600
RM	80%	360		80%	480
Gross Profits		90			120
Overheads		80			75
Profits		10			45
Profit %		2%			8%

Example Two: Forging Unit

Operations in a quality and price sensitive environment, focus needs to be on process excellence and quality

A forging plant in Europe had 90% of its sales coming from a single customer based out of two plants in Italy and France. Different products were being supplied to these plants, rollers to the Italian plant, and track links to the French plant. Defect rates were close to 10% and the customer was extremely unhappy with this, and had reduced the company's business share from 80% to 50% as a result. They were further threatening to close down buying altogether.

What did we do:

1. Introduce rigid 100% pre dispatch inspection. This eliminated defects to a large extent at the customer's end, but did not solve the internal problem of wastage and high costs.

2. Analyze each step of the manufacturing process, and identify where and why defects were being generated.

3. Identify the root cause of defect generation and eliminate it.

4. Measure process capability Cpk of each process and make sure it exceeded 1.67. *(Process capability Index (Cpk) is a statistical tool, to measure the ability of a process to produce output within customer's specification limits. In simple words, it measures producer's capability to produce a product within customer's tolerance range. Cpk is used to estimate how close you are to a given target and how consistent you are to around your average performance. Cpk gives you the best-case scenario for the existing process. It can also estimate future process performance, assuming performance is consistent over time.)*

5. Eliminate the 100% pre dispatch inspection in slow stages.

Take a look at the comparison below to see outcome:

	Before			After	
	Qty	**Value**		**Qty**	**Value**
Production	100	1000		100	1000
Sales	90	900		100	1000
Scrap	10	10		0	0
Net Sales		910			1000
RM		650			650
Gross Profits		260			350
Overheads		180			150*
Net profits		80			200
Net profits %		8.8%			20.0%

* Overheads reduced due to lesser amount of rework and the savings in getting the rejected material back from the customers place for rework.

Additional benefits of the above were that the customer was so happy that they increased the company's share of business to 80% again. Our Management was also felicitated at a special function at the customer's plant in France. But that's another story.

Example Three: Consumer Durables

Fund mismanagement, leading to suppliers declining to supply consistently, leading to loss of production and sales, progressively leading to losses

A large auto components and white goods manufacturing company had become sick due to progressive mismanagement of funds. This was compounded by the banks cutting of working capital limits, declaring the company as NPA, and finally the company went into Reconstruction. This happened in spite of the company having excellent state of the art manufacturing facilities.

What did we do:

1. The Promoter MD was replaced by a professional MD with market credibility, which the promoters had lost.

2. A supplier's conference was convened by the new MD and suppliers were assured that they would be paid for current supplies in 30 days without fail provided they resumed supplies. Additionally, they were promised that old outstanding amounts would be cleared at 8% per month, so that in a year they would be all stabilized at 30 days clean credit without any old dues pending. After a lot of discussion (the meeting lasted all day), 95% of the suppliers agreed.

3. A workers' meeting was also convened and an incentive of INR 2/- per component was offered for all production over 70% of the installed capacity. This was received very well by the employees and production ramped up steeply, because supplies of inputs had also resumed.

4. Banks were roped in and their support sought and obtained for the scheme of reconstruction.

A simple case of taking the bull by the horns and applying soft skills to the situation resulted in a dramatic change. Take a look at the outcome:

	Before			After	
	Qty	**Value**		**Qty**	**Value**
Sales	40	400		100	1000
RM	60%	240		60%	600
Gross Profits		160			400
Overheads		200			220
Net profits		-40			180
Net profits %		-10.0%			18.0%

This is an instance when a counter intuitive decision to actually increase the overhead cost by paying production linked incentive was taken in order to revive the company.

Example Four: Healthcare Services

Service organization with declining Revenues due to poor levels of service

This case is that of a famous high-end hospital, which also performs a lot of charitable surgeries as well as paid high-end surgeries and treatment. Patient footfalls were declining, as were revenues from diagnostics and surgery, and the hospital was fast approaching distress levels.

What did we do:

As a new CEO, the obvious first step was to assess the problem. Some of the problems were fairly obvious:

1. Casual and sloppy attitude of the paramedics.

2. Doctors prescribing unnecessary diagnostic tests which were expensive (out of which they get a percentage as incentive)

3. Very high waiting time for patients, both first time patients and repeat patients.

A few simple measures were taken:

1. Paramedics were provided a balanced score card with targets for each stage of patient care, from registration, check-up, doctor referral, diagnostics, and follow up. Department heads were required to report their performance versus target on a daily basis on a white board maintained in the department, and it was made clear to them that increments of the team members would depend entirely on their performance.

2. Doctor's income including incentive or commission earnings was calculated over the previous three months. We averaged

that, added 10% to their salaries, and fixed that as a salary, eliminating incentive. They were also told that future increments would depend on quality of care rather than on quantity. This is a counter intuitive measure, but when one thinks about it, patient footfall depends on word of mouth feedback by patients to others. Good care automatically results in more patient visits. Since the doctors were not now interested in unnecessary prescription of diagnostics, care improved, machine utilization became better, stress levels were lower, and care improved dramatically.

3. Surgery rates were rationalized with prices reduced for cheaper surgeries and increased for very high-end sophisticated surgeries. The logic here was that wealthy patients could afford to pay more, whereas lower end patients needed quality eye care at reasonable cost. Overall, this resulted in an increase in revenue rather than decrease.

4. A small initiative: every visiting patient was offered a cup of hot coffee. This may sound like a small thing, but it is surprising how much difference it made.

5. A digital board was set up, showing the patient his turn number, and the estimated waiting time in minutes. Overall, throughput time for a patient was reduced from 175 minutes earlier to 40 minutes. This figure is in line with global best practices. As a matter of interest, almost all the well-known hospitals in India started offering coffee to patients after this initiative. Not all achieved the same results, because they did not do the other things along with the coffee.

The Outcome:

Within a year, revenue grew 60% and EBIDTA doubled. Need we say more?

Example Five: A Metal Company

Facing stiff competition from Cheap Chinese Products.

A large integrated aluminum company was facing heavy competition from Chinese products, due to Government policy of zero import duty. In some instances, Chinese products like extruded aluminum sections were available at lower price than the manufacturing cost of the company. Consequent loss of sales, leading to fiscal losses, and the Company did not know what to do about it.

We had a single mandate - to revive the organization by any legal means possible. What did we do?

Assessment of the problem showed two or three different symptoms:

1. The company was operating at 60% capacity utilization due to lack of orders.

2. The RM cost to sales was 85% due to low pricing, rather than due to high input costs. Despite this low price, sales were still low because the Chinese material was still cheaper.

3. Discussions with dealers showed that they would prefer the locally manufactured material rather than Chinese product if the prices were matched.

4. Assessment of the Chinese product showed two things:

   a) The gauge of the extrusion was lighter (1.2 mm on average instead of 1.6 mm). Hence the cost per length was lower.

   b) The brittleness of the extrusion was much higher than the local product. This indicated that substantial amount of scrap metal was being used in the raw material, as opposed to what the African company was doing, using virgin ingot. This also impacted the cost.

14

Decisions taken and implemented included the following:

1. Dies were procured from China to manufacture extrusion in 1.2 mm thickness.

2. A large purchase team (16 people) was constituted solely to purchase scrap aluminum domestically as well as from the neighboring nations with whom there was a trade treaty. This scrap was melted, mixed with virgin aluminum in a ratio of 40:60, molded into billets, and used for extrusion production.

3. Continuous motivation and training was given to the team, who were quite disheartened and depressed, not having received increments in the past three years. This included walkarounds on a daily basis by the MD, with stops at operator stations to chat, improvement in canteen services, organizing a football tournament, having an in-house medical dispensary, and many other small initiatives aimed at improving employee morale.

The outcome:

	Before			After	
	Qty	**Value**		**Qty**	**Value**
Sales	60	600		95	950
RM	80%	480		65%	618
Gross Profits		120			332
Overheads		200			200
Net profits		-80			132
Net profits %		-13.3%			13.9%

Once it became clear that it was possible to compete with and beat the Chinese, the Company availed loans to purchase two more extrusion presses (ironically, from China), and further increased the plant capacity, to increasingly boost profits.

Example Six: A Restaurant Chain

Lost controls in growing too fast too soon.

A 13-year-old Restaurant Chain with about 12 outlets was in financial trouble due to lack of controls and no measurement of financial data. The costing was nonexistent and the data was not recorded at all. They were bleeding and had no idea how to turn it around.

Assessment of the problem showed three major problems:

1. Non-availability of Data recording and analysis.

2. Product pricing, promotional spends, etc. was done on a gut-feel.

3. Mis-reading the trends in terms of impact of food aggregators and delivery platforms (Swiggy, Zomato and Uber-Eats) on Business.

Decisions taken and implemented included the following:

1. Accounting and Finance Team was strengthened and a monthly MIS instituted for each outlet and for the company as a whole. MIS included not only revenues but also the analysis of all the expenses so that any abnormal expense jump can be identified and then appropriate actions can be taken to control the same.

2. Biggest cost being food costs, strict portion control measures were instituted and the entire cooking staff trained and re-trained in the same.

3. Prices were increased 3 times in six months. The new prices were about 40% higher than the old prices (which have not been revised for more than 3 years. Contrary to expectations,

the sales volume also increased by 10% even after this price rise as we had more money for marketing and promotions.

4.   A few unprofitable stores were closed down permanently.

5.   Data became the backbone of all decisions.

The Results were

	Before			After	
	Qty	Value		Qty	Value
Sales	60	600		70	980
Food Costs	55%	330		40%	392
Gross Profits		270			588
Overheads		350			375
Aggregator commissions		54			102.9
Net profits		-134			110.1
Net profits %		-22.3%			11.2%

Not only were we able to increase sales volumes, the increased pricing gave us much better margins and bought us back to profitability.

Increasing prices to get more sales was a bit counter-intuitive, but it did work out.

Summary

The common thread running through all these cases, is that they are the result of progressive management inaction or wrong action over time, which results in a situation which the management then finds to be untenable. The solutions are relatively simple, in many cases quite obvious, but the management is unable to see these solutions. Even if they do, they perceive it as "risk", and lack both the skill and the will to implement the solutions.

Good leadership and objective, dispassionate assessment and action, is the key to success.

One disclaimer here is that not all turnaround efforts succeed (most will if the problems are diagnosed correctly and on time). Delay in diagnosis or wrong diagnosis will surely lead a very high chance of the business closing down.

Now that you have seen a few examples and you may also have found something in there which really resonates, the next question is how to identify what the problem is. What the real reason is? The next section is specifically dedicated for identifying the issues.

PART II: Diagnosing the Problem

A lot of people will be scared about this step. Most of the entrepreneurs out there will simply ignore the problems and go about their daily work as if it does not exist. Most of them will go on with the hope that one day, the problem will resolve itself. Are you one of them?

As Entrepreneurs, most of us know instinctively that things are not going right. But a lot of times, the inbuilt optimism overshadows the concerns and they are just forgotten till the time they become really bad. One needs to avoid doing this and start by accepting that there is a problem.

Is it really so hard to know if your business is facing troubles? And how can we objectively decide if our business is functioning properly or not? How do we identify the problem areas and what needs work on?

Let's take the example of a doctor or a physician - If you go to a doctor, he will ask you for symptoms, take your weight, blood pressure, run a couple of tests, and then after the reports come in, will give you a final diagnosis.

We also have a similar process.

1. Gather all information – financial information, audit reports, bank statements, stock statements etc. for the last 3 years.

2. Ask the right questions and get facts to answer most of them.

3. Reach a diagnosis.

Each step is elaborated in the following pages. We promise you that if you follow the 3-steps diligently, it will give an absolutely clear picture of what is going wrong in your business.

Step One: Gather Information

Gathering information is essentially collecting all the historical data (just as a doctor collects your medical history) needed to properly answer the questions that will follow. Indicative list of documents will include the following: -

1. Financials for the last 3 years – Including profit and loss accounts, balance sheets, and audit reports.

2. Bank Statements and loan statements for the last 3 years.

3. Details related to production – Customer Rejection rates, overtime paid, process charts, inventory and stock statements, scrap sale reports, plant and equipment utilization rates (one/ two / three shift operations), rejection reports, etc.

4. Feedback from Employees, Customers, Bankers, Suppliers etc.

This remains a very critical step as if the data is not available or is wrong, then the chances of a mis-diagnosis is very high. If the Problems are not identified correctly, they will never be solved. Worse still, you may spend your efforts and resources on solving the wrong problems or problems which are not there only.

We would suggest that you gather all the information in one place (a file or a computer) so that when time comes to ask questions, you have the data readily available for assessment.

Step Two: Ask the Right Questions

This is a list of questions which every business owner or management needs to ask and answer as objectively as possible. The answers will directly point to weaknesses in the business, and solutions will become suddenly visible.

Spend some time on this section answering all the questions in details with numbers and data. This is of utmost importance and the entire purpose of you picking up this book will be defeated if you ignore this step.

Let's get on with the Questions now. We suggest that You first answer the question in a YES or NO. Then, you also will write down the details, numbers, etc. after that.

We very strongly urge you to answer all the questions and then spend some time analyzing those answers. There will be a lot of light bulbs going on.

I. **CORPORATE MANAGEMENT AND STRATEGY:**
   1. Do you have a structured 5-year business plan detailing product sales, markets, likely costs, opportunities and risks?
   2. Do you have a detailed budget for every fiscal year, which is prepared at the end of the previous year?
   3. Is this budget detailed into monthly and weekly time slots?
   4. Do you plan for and make provisions for capital expenditure?
   5. Do you have a performance Management system in place, and is it implemented objectively?
   6. Do you track market trends and adjust your future strategy in order to maximize opportunities in any scenario?
   7. Do you know who is your competition and what are they doing? Financials as well as non-financial information?

8. Do You know about the size of your market and whether it is growing or not?

II. **SALES AND MARKETING:**
1. Do you know the sales trends of last 3 years?
2. Do you know the monthly sales trends for the last 12 months?
3. Do you have an interactive website?
4. Do you track sales product-wise and value wise on a daily or weekly basis?
5. Do you know which your top selling products in terms of contribution to your total sales are (10%)?
6. Do you know which products are the least contributing to overall sales (bottom 10%)?
7. Do you have a plan in place to phase out your weakest products?
8. Do you know which of the products you sell have the best gross margins? And the products which have the least gross margins?

III. **MANUFACTURING/PRODUCTION:**
1. Do you manufacture for inventory or do you manufacture against orders?
2. Are all your product lines manufacturing to full capacity?
3. Is your product defect rate greater than 1%?
4. Do you have a system of process capability analysis and do you work continuously on improving process capability?
5. Are you conscious and aware of the seven types of waste in an organization (transportation, inventory, motion, waiting, over processing, overproduction, and defects)?
6. Is your production (and sales) inconsistent, varying significantly (>25%) month to month?
7. Do you do kaizens (small continuous improvements) to eliminate the above?

IV.   PURCHASE AND LOGISTICS:

1. Do you have an ERP or other computerized system to maintain inventories?
2. Do you categorize your inventory into A, B, and C categories? Are you aware that A category items constitute 20% of the quantity of inventory but 80% of the value?
3. Do you follow a system of FIFO? (First in first out)
4. Does your Purchase team have a cost reduction target which you monitor on a regular basis?
5. Do you have a logistics service provider, and are you aware of the cost of logistics as a percentage of sales? Do you charge the customer for packaging and freight?

V.   CASH FLOW:

1. Does your finance department prepare a cash flow statement on a weekly basis (current plus next week's projection)?
2. What is your debtor's to turnover ratio? Is it less than 20%?
3. What is your inventory to turnover ratio? Is it less than 20%?
4. Do you have a structured system of tracking debtors' aging and regular reminding of customers for payment?
5. Do you pay your suppliers as per the negotiated credit period?
6. Are you able to pay your lenders and employees on time, every-time?

VI   PRODUCTIVITY:

1. What is your sales per employee? Is it at least seven times the salary you pay?
2. Do you have any measure for employee productivity?
3. Do you have a Daily Work sheet system for your employees, which is tracked by your Production Managers?
4. Do you have an organization for customer service and support?

5. Do you have a system for analysis and rectification of customer complaints? Do you do root cause analysis to eliminate the reason for a problem?
6. Are you overburdening some people in your organization while others are not loaded sufficiently?

VII   MANAGEMENT AND CULTURE:

1. Are you a leader or a boss? Do you demand respect from your employees or do you earn it by your behavior and actions?
2. Do you insist that your employees give respect and courtesy to each other?
3. Do you have an equitable gender ratio? Do you have a documented HR Policy in place, which includes a Sexual Harassment policy?
4. Do you have a system in place to address employee grievances?
5. Do you have Health Insurance for your employees? Keyman Insurance for important employees?
6. Do you have a system of incentivizing good ideas of your employees?

In the next section, we will give you a small technique on how to draw conclusions about what ails your business basis the answers to the questions above.

Step Three: Diagnosis

Now that you have answered all the questions above, we would want you to notice that we have conveniently divided the section above in 7 different buckets or sections.

More number of No's you have in a section (absolute number – two, three, four, five, etc.), the more that particular part of business needs attention and work. The section with the Highest number of No's takes first priority with the section with the second highest number of No's taking second priority and so on and so forth.

Simple. Isn't it?

Yes, there will be multiple battles to fight, but you need to prioritize which ones to fight first. Fighting all the battles together is a sure recipe of disaster.

We suggest that you tackle only 2 parts from the list above at any point of time. At the most 3 parts. Never More.

Our Personal Experience says that the biggest and the most immediate improvements can be had by working on Sales and Marketing and Cash Flow Issues of the company.

PART III: The Prescription

I will like to start this section with the words of someone great –

I don't like my mind right now
Stacking up problems that are so unnecessary
Wish that I could slow things down
I wanna let go but there's comfort in the panic
And I drive myself crazy
Thinking everything's about me
Yeah, I drive myself crazy
'Cause I can't escape the gravity
I'm holding on
Why is everything so heavy?

Now Read that again. And one more time please. Let the words sink in. Isn't it your state of mind right now?

Now you know what ails your business and the extent of the ailment, and you also know all the problems and stress that you are carrying around.

What follows here is the prescription. We have divided this into 2 parts – A Emergency Procedure when things are extremely dire and a slightly longer-term slow cure to get back to health – totally and completely.

But you have to understand one thing. The first one is just the emergency procedure to ensure that the patient survives. For long term health, you need to treat all the other ailments – However big or small they may be.

With that out of the way, Let's get into each one of them.

p.s. If you really want to know who said these words above, It is a song released in 2017 by Linkin Park. Do check it out.

Chapter One: The Emergency Procedure

Every entrepreneur sees times when business is at its absolute bottom. When they often wonder how to keep the doors of the business open and the production ongoing. Times when they wonder how to pay salaries and how will they pay the bankers.

In times of such dire trouble, focus on the 7 steps below to ensure immediate survival and to ensure that the mortal threat to the business goes away:

1. Try to maximize revenue rather than cut costs.
2. Prioritize collection of funds.
3. Renegotiate credit with suppliers
4. Identify loss making products (even if they have very low positive margins, they take up capacity which could be better used by higher margin products) and stop making them.
5. Put aside 10% of every inflow into a contingency fund.
6. Maintain a good relationship with your bank. Even in bad times, if the bank has confidence in you, they will likely support you.
7. Hang in there, do the right things, and the situation will invariably improve.

Let's look at each one of them in a little detail.

1. Try to maximize revenue rather than cut costs.

Increasing sales and revenues is much easier in the short term than cutting costs and increasing efficiencies.

Assuming that you are doing business with positive gross margins, and considering that lack of funds and profits is the primary reason for any kind of stress in business, increasing sales which are gross margin positive is the simplest way to improve one's condition. Consider the following example –

	Before			After	
	Qty	Value		Qty	Value
Sales	40	400		60	600
RM	60%	240		60%	360
Gross Profits		160			240
Overheads / fixed expenses		200			200
Net profits		-40			40
Net profits %		-10.0%			6.7%

As you can see, by doing nothing else but increasing sales, you can get from a situation of losses and distress to profits. And is it very difficult to increase this? Not really. It's a matter of focus, process and effort. Do the following things and your sales will surely go up in a very short span of time: -

a. Have a defined and robust sales process – The Sales Funnel Process works every time.

b. Have a focused and motivated sales team. If needed, strengthen your sales team.

c. Institute an incentive plan for your sales team (if there is no such plan already).

d. Set clear sales target for the teams and equip them with the necessary tools.

e. Review, Review and Review: - Measure all aspects of your sales process (No of customers contacted, the conversion ratio, the reason for losing a customer, etc.)

f.   Increase the number of clients and increase the value of each sale.

g.   Ensure that your plan also includes reaching out ex-customers who no longer work with us and win them again.

2.   Prioritize collection of funds.

You need cash to pay salaries. You need Cash to buy inventories. You need Cash to pay for electricity. You need cash to get the finished product transported to your customer. You need cash to repay bankers and lenders.

And you need this even more when things are more challenging, when things are very difficult. When you are behind on your bills, when salaries are overdue.

The only solution to this is to collect faster from your customers. How do you do this? Simple steps –

a.   Asking your customer for faster payments and even advances along with orders.

b.   Doing more business with customers who pay faster.

c.   Offering cash discounts to current debtors and receivables (even if it means that you lose your profits on the transaction).

d.   Settling with disputed receivables – even at 40%-50% of the amounts claimed, if so needed.

And No, borrowing more is not the solution for additional cash flows. You are unable to afford current cash outflow; how will you afford the outflows of the additional outflow on account of the new debt?

3. Renegotiate credit with suppliers

Increasing sales and collecting money faster will help you with more cash inflows. This next step applies particularly to manufacturing industries and not service businesses.

Typically, the largest purchase (40%-85% of sales) is purchases of raw material to produce the final goods. A simple way to dramatically improve your cash flows is to renegotiate credit period with your vendors. Even if you get your vendors to increase the credit period from 30 days to 60 days, you suddenly have additional cash flow of about 8.33% of your purchases as additional working capital magically.

Add this with the additional cash inflows on account of faster collection and (maybe) additional sales, will mean that suddenly you will have additional surplus cash left over at the end of the month. This can be then used to pay off older debts, build capacities, invest in equipment's etc.

There can be a situation where your suppliers are already stretched and you are delayed in paying your dues. Even in such a case, you need to try to get some concessions from your existing suppliers.

If it works and your existing suppliers support you, good. Else, you simply find alternate suppliers. Your Business survival takes priority.

4. **Identify loss making products and stop making them.**

This is the most basic. You cannot get ahead if you are walking backwards. You cannot heal and get healthy if you keep bleeding.

This also applies for products with low positive margins. They take up capacity which could be better used by higher margin products.

Do this even if this means that you will lose 50%-60% of your business. It's absolute no brainer.

5. **Put aside 10% of every inflow into a contingency fund.**

This is very counter-intuitive and works on the principle of pay yourself first. You will immediately think – I do not have enough cash flow to service my current outflows and liabilities, where will I get this additional 10% from? The temptation to just take it and pay a vendor who is sitting on your head or to the banker who is after your life to pay the overdues interest will be too great.

The Presumption is that you have a negative cash flow at this point and are already working on increasing your sales and plugging that cash flow gap.

But we have a few solid reasons to do put that 10% away –

a. If you are already in a hole every month, a little more pressure every month will not really impact you much. If You are able to manage with 100, you will be able to make do with 90.

b. Keeping 10% of money collected every month (presuming that you collect 100%) in a separate bank account will mean that at the end of the year, you will have an amount equivalent to 8.33% of your turnover in the bank.

c. Having some money accumulate in your bank account every month is a great psychological boost.

d. This will act as an emergency fund to be used in case of real emergencies (like the present COVID-19 pandemic where the businesses are totally shut down).

6. **Maintain a good relationship with your bank.**

A banker has as much stake in your business as you. At times, they have a larger interest too (every heard of debt-equity ratio and most of the times it is 3:1 or more).

They have supported you in good times and have increased your financing limit every time you needed funds. Now, even in bad times, if the bank has confidence in you, they will likely support you and help you in your recovery too.

Keep them updated of all your efforts, the plans and the execution updates. Keep them updated of your increasing cash flows. Within the rules of the land, the bankers also would want you to recover and will help you more often than not. They may not extend further cash limits, but they will certainly help by not taking or delaying strong recovery actions.

7. **Hang in there, do the right things, and the situation will invariably improve.**

This will be a difficult time and a difficult process to handle. There will be days when the bankers will not listen to you, there will be days when suppliers will give you problems and there will be days when everything will appear insurmountable.

But you have to stay optimistic and positive during these tough times. Have faith. Every night is followed by a day. If I have to quote from one of my favorite songs of all times, it will say –

I've paid my dues
Time after time
I've done my sentence
But committed no crime
And bad mistakes
I've made a few
I've had my share of sand kicked in my face
But I've come through
We are the champions, my friends
And we'll keep on fighting 'til the end

> *We are the champions*
> *We are the champions*
> *No time for losers*
> *'Cause we are the champions of the world*

"We are the Champions – Queen."

Now that we have looked at the emergency procedure, let's look at the steps needed for a sustainable turnaround of business.

Chapter Two: The Long and Only Road to Health

You have already identified what is ailing your business (all the things that you said NO to in one of the previous sections of the book). The more the number of NO's, the more problems needs addressing. For the sake of convenience, we have again classified the possible actions needed into the same 7 groups as earlier. Without further delays, lets dive straight into this and

I. MANAGEMENT AND STRATEGY:

1. Stop Fooling Yourself.

We have discussed something called a "Blind Management Syndrome" earlier. Most of the Business owners and leaders we meet cannot see glaring mistakes and issues which are right in front of them. A lot of times they are also in denial mode (we are not wrong, its them, it's the market, it's the economy, it's the bankers, but it is never me). The First thing which every management needs to do is to look into the mirror and accept the following 2 facts-

a. That things and processes and decisions went wrong and the business is ailing.
b. Things will not become better on their own. The business will not recover on its own.

Once you accept that there are problems and issues, then you can go about solving them.

2. Do the opposite of what your Gut tells you (90% of the times)

There is a scientific reason behind this suggestion. Our Gut feeling or intuition is basically the programmed experiences of millions of years of evolution and is based on a basic instinct of survival. The underlying factor which contributes to it is fear. While it was helpful in prehistoric ages when it actually aided in our survival against the elements and wild animals, it is of very little use in making business decisions today when there is no mortal threat to us personally.

In stressful conditions like financial stress, dropping sales, etc, the primary feeling driving your intuition will be fear and anxiety.

Once present, anxiety and fear have important implications on one's decision-making. First, anxiety increases how much information individuals seek out and can lead to analysis paralysis.

Anxiety and fear may also directly influence the decisions individuals make. They increase risk aversion, leading individuals to choose safer paths of action. They also make individuals less likely to take action at all, with the most common response being withdrawal and passivity.

All of the above are not good when there is action and quick decision making needed.

3. Prepare a detailed business plan.

Do you have a detailed business plan for the next 5 years? Detailed down to Profit and Loss accounts, Balance Sheets, Monthly and quarterly sales projections, cost projections, people requirement and financial ratios?

If not then, I have news for you my friend. The Business will not grow at all or even it grows, it will grow in fits and starts? You will not think of driving with a blindfold on, will you?

A plan will help you know what you want to achieve and then plan your activity levels accordingly. Let's take an example. Let's see how you will plan a sales activity:

If You don't have a business Plan?

- You will not know what sales targets are to be given to your sales managers.
- You will not be able to plan your sales activities and promotions around it as you do not know what sales number do you want to achieve.
- You will not be able to plan training sessions for your people (as you do not know what is the end result expected from them).
- You will not be able to devise incentive plans for the team as you will not be able to measure if they have underperformed or overperformed.
- Each member of your team worries about the long-term growth of his career. If you do not give them a

clearly defined path, how will they be secure about the long-term prospects within the company?

You see, it's not a very good way to do business.

Now consider the case where you have a clearly defined 5-year plan. In this case, you will be able to:

- Clearly set the sales targets for each member of your sales team.
- Clearly devise training programs and incentive plans.
- Decide on the tools and training needed basis the clearly defined sales targets.
- Have a clear career path for a sales manager to grow with the company.

This will also help you prioritize your resources. Whatever is planned to achieve in the next 6-8 months will get priority and so on and so forth. You should not worry about what is planned for next year.

Apply this thought to other processes and parts of your business. Ask yourself the question – Do you have a plan of action for production – be it purchases, people or processes? Do you have a plan for debt repayment? Do you have plan to build cash reserves? Do you have a plan for new product development?

Do you have plans for the situation wherein your largest customer suddenly stops giving you business or goes bankrupt? Do you have plans for contingencies, emergencies and eventualities?

Planning exists for a reason; if we refuse to plan, we run the risk of having completely and totally unanticipated things happen.

So, what constitutes a business plan? We will list down below the essential parts that your Business Plan must contain: -

1. Financial Plan – This includes the Profit and Loss Account and the Balance Sheets along with all calculations and assumptions.

2. Competition and market analysis – Data and information on you direct and indirect competitors. You should also include the market analysis for your product within this plan (Is it a growing market, or a price sensitive market?).

3. Contingency Plans – Think of difficult situations and unpredictable scenarios and then plan your course of action for each of them. They may never happen, but it's like insurance. You take it and pray that you will never have to use the same.

4. It is broken down into smaller and smaller plans for each function and team of your business. For example, the larger business plan will lead to preparation of sales plan, purchase plans and human resources plan.

5. They are further broken down into monthly and weekly plans of action. You cannot eat an elephant in one sitting. But, if you eat a small portion every day, very soon you will finish the elephant. Same goes for a business also. You break down the annual plan into small bite sized components and then ensure that you finish those smaller tasks.

So, what are you waiting for? If you do not already have a business plan, make one now. Please also involve your senior team also in making of this business plan. If you are not comfortable with the numbers or drawing up financials, appoint a professional.

A well drafted Business Plan will change the way you do your business and will ensure that the whole operation turns around and gets its jump start towards profits and sustainability.

4. Review, Review and Review

You have made your business plans, but they will be of no use if they remain in your laptop and are never referred to again.

Regular reviews can help with the following: -

a. Identifying problems and issues early and then solving them at the very beginning.
b. Doing mid-term course corrections.
c. Identifying training needs – to facilitate better performance.
d. Increasing employee engagement.

Most of the businesses We know do not have any review system in place. And at the end of the year, they suddenly find themselves in wide variance with the targets in revenues, profits and even costs (they are normally more than planned).

This will not normally happen if you do regular reviews and then focus on activities and functions which are underperforming.

II.   SALES AND MARKETING:

1. Stop selling loss making and low margin products.

It's a simple concept really. You cannot come out of the hole if you keep digging. The first thing which you need to do is to STOP DIGGING. Stop selling products which have negative gross margins or low gross margins. It will have the following effect on your business: -

a. Your losses will be controlled immediately. See the example below

	Before				After		
	Prod. A	Prod. B	Company Total		Prod. A	Prod. B	Company Total
Sales	100	100	200		100	0	100
Raw Material Cost (%)	65%	90%			65%	90%	
Raw Material Cost value	65	90	155		65	0	65
Processing Cost (%)	10%	10%			10%	10%	
Processing Cost value	15	15	30		10	0	10
Total Cost to manufacture excl. Labour	80	105	185		80	0	80
Gross Margins	20	-5	15		20	0	20
Other Fixed Overheads incl labour			15				15
Net Margins			0				5

You can run any example. In every single case, cutting out a loss-making product will only improve your margins.

b. You will release production capacities for other products with better margins.

2. Make it a science with defined process.

a. *Sales Funnels.*

It is a simple process of measuring and understanding the sales process in terms of contacting the customer (Awareness), Converting him to a prospect (Interest), Helping him decide (Decision) and closing the same (Action or Closing).

The process says that for every 100 customers you contact, at every stage you will lose customers and, in the end, anywhere between 2-5 prospects will become actual customers.

The basis of the sales funnel is measuring the activity during each step and ensuring that the process is followed.

b. *Measure your sales activity and every step of the sales conversion process.*

It's important to measure the number of customers lost at each stage of the funnel and the reason thereof. If you have this measurement in place, you can with a certain amount of certainty estimate your sales volumes basis the number of customers contacted.

The second benefit is that If you can address some objections, you can improve the overall conversion rates and hence increase the sales volume without incurring additional costs.

3. *Increase your sales efforts at least by a multiple of 5.*

Now you are not selling loss making and low margin products and you also have your sales funnel working. How do you increase sales next?

Simple, by increasing the amount of effort put in the process and that too in the first step of the sales funnel. If you have a final conversion ratio of 5%, 100 customer contacts will give you 5 sales and 500 customer contacts will give you 25 sales.

It is basic mathematics and it is here that a lot of organizations fail. They work on fancy projects to increase conversions and to train their sales people on some fancy new technique o approaching a customer. Most of them will not work. What will surely work is the extra effort put in the sales funnel.

4. Focus your selling efforts on 4% of the products:

I am sure you have heard of the Pareto principle. 20% of the products will give you about 80% of the profits. This is true in most of the organizations and for most of the functions too.

However, For sales process, we take this a step further and apply the Pareto principle twice. You will find that approximately 4% of your products will bring in 60%-65% margins. Even if you focus on increasing sales of these 4% products which bring in bulk of your profits, you can easily scale up your revenues and margins in a very short amount of time.

III. MANUFACTURING/PRODUCTION:

1. *Don't handle any item more than once.*

One of the most glaring yet overlooked mistakes in any production process is overhandling of items. Each time you pick up an item and keep it somewhere else, it is a cost in terms of time taken, manpower and equipment's used. Please study all your processes. Ensure that the material flow is Receipt > Store > Production Floor and no more.

Same goes for handling Finished Goods too. Ideal should be Production Floor > Dispatch. But is that does not work, then it should be Production Floor > Storage > Dispatch. Not one step extra.

It also applies to service industries too. Please ensure that all tasks are handled only once and not multiple times. Streamline the process and do not go to a task again and again.

2. *Optimize each process –*

Review each production process in details. If needed, appoint professionals who can help you with a process audit and improvements. Often you are using old processes and the number of steps and the time taken to complete them can be reduced to a great extent by use of newer equipment's and maybe newer materials.

Cutting out 1 step from a 4-step process is a 25% saving in manpower costs. Each step cut from the process is a reduction in errors and mistakes. Though, it looks very small, the compound effect of this can be very far reaching when you work in very high volumes.

3. *Redesign and Improve Your Production Flow*

A poor production flow will lead to worker fatigue, excessive handling of material, poor quality and loss of time and effort. Redesigning the production flow so that it flows smoothly and without speed-breakers is very important.

A smooth process flow can also lead to better and efficient space utilization and may create additional space for expansion within the same premises.

Have a look at your process flow. How can you improve it?

4. Invest in Better Equipment's

Finding finance to buy equipment's is not the easiest thing to do when a business is in distress.

But if the machinery is old, it will invariably be inefficient and labor intensive. There are a lot of new generation equipment's which give you twice the production with half the labor force, and also better quality.

If you cannot afford to buy a completely new equipment's, can you get some add-on process equipment to make your production process more efficient than what it is at present?

Older equipment's will have more downtime compared to newer well-maintained equipment's again affecting the throughput and the production capacity.

5. ***One Counter-intuitive thought: Technology is not the Answer to Everything***

Automation and new technology normally improve efficiencies and are better for quality. However, it is not always advisable. Why do we say this?

Automating a wrong process will mean that now you are doing wrong automatically which earlier you were doing wrong manually.

Read the earlier sentence again please.

What we are saying is we should first focus on making your existing process right and efficient. Once we have done that, then automate by all means.

6. ***Best in Class Preventive Maintenance***

Is your maintenance schedule a reactive process? If your production often hampered due to equipment breakdowns? Are you spending a lot of time, money and resources on repairs?

If yes, then you will be facing the following:

a. Higher downtimes (of the equipment and the production line) due to equipment breakdowns which leads to drop in production.

b. Higher maintenance costs which directly impact the profits.

c. Shortening the life of the equipment in some cases.

The best companies have a world class preventive maintenance schedule which ensures that the equipment's and facilities are always in the best possible condition. This not only ensures maximum uptime, but also lesser maintenance costs and enhanced equipment life. If you do not have a planned maintenance schedule, ensure that you make and implement one today.

IV.   PURCHASE AND LOGISTICS:

Are there a few periods when you do not have space to store the inventory and some periods where your production comes to a halt due to lack of inventory? If you have answered in yes to the above question, then your inventory management systems and processes need an overhaul.

You can start by simple answering the following questions: -

1. *Do you have an ERP or other computerized system to maintain inventories?*

A few questions to ask yourself here are:

- How to you record the movement of inventory?
- Is it still manual registers or is it a basic excel sheet?
- Do you have a proper inventory management software? (even tally has a competent inventory module, if used properly)
- Are you using the software properly and generating value added reports like Re-order Levels, Re-order Quantities, Cost Data, inventory holding levels etc. from the software on a regular basis?
- Are you reviewing this data regularly?

What is needed is a properly configured inventory management system with the following things measured and controlled by the system: -

- Control over entire inventory and its value.
- Production Costs or Cost of Goods Sold.
- Re-order levels

- Re-order quantities
- Inventory price trends and variances over a period of time.

When you will have all the data above, you can take informed decisions about your production process as well as cost analysis.

2. *Optimizing the inventory holding levels*

What is the optimum inventory level? It is defined by the lead time it takes for your supplier to send you a particular part with some cushion added to it for safety.

For example, your steel supplier sends you material one week after ordering, then you should keep about 10 days of steel in stock (7 days the supply time + 3 days buffer) to ensure continuous production.

Anything more than 10 days is un-necessary wastage of working capital (inventory in your warehouse and not being used is of no value). That money is better used elsewhere for either buying some other required inventory or to reduce your working capital utilization and resultant saving of interest. Also, you will save the space needed to store excess inventories.

Anything less than 10 days and you are risking the chance of your production lines stopping due to any kind of shortage of raw material. Any event like breakdown at supplier's place, transporters strike, curfews etc. can derail your production.

V.   CASH FLOW:

The most important parameter of a business is its cash flow. Not Profit, Not Net Worth, but cash flow. You might be insanely profitable, but if you are not able to collect that money, you will still default on your loan repayments. To improve your cash flows, you can take the following steps: -

1. *Prepare a weekly cash flow statement*

If you can, you should measure it on a daily basis. If that is not possible, then a weekly measurement is a must.

Does your finance department prepare a cash flow statement on a weekly basis (current plus next week's projection)? Can you tell us with reasonable certainty the collection which you will do next week and the expenses which are due for payment? Can you tell us with confidence, the surplus or shortfall in cash which had this week and which you expect in the coming week?

If not, then, I am afraid my friend, you are running your business on a hope and a prayer. And there is a very strong likelihood that your business will be facing periods of absolute cash crunches and then periods of outlandish cash surpluses.

Start by preparing a weekly cash flow statement and you will see an amazing difference in a few weeks itself.

And now you are measuring your cash flows, let's go about improving it.

2. Increase collections

The most basic way to improve cash flows is to increase your collections. It includes the following: -

- **Increasing sales**

  Increasing sales will obviously mean an increased collection. The more you sell, the more you collect. Do you really need any more explanation on this?

- **Sales at better collection terms.**

  Selling more only is not enough. Can you sell at better terms? Can you sell in cash instead of credit? Can you reduce the credit period to 30 days instead of 60 days? Can you ask for an advance along with the order? Can you collect today by offering cash discounts? Think about how can you collect the money faster.

- **Current Overdue Debtors**

  One major point which a lot of businesses struggle with is what to do with existing overdue collections. What to do with clients who are not paying and what to do with client who have issues and disputes? There are a few things which you can and absolutely must do and collect the money as soon as possible: -

  - Settle with them and collect the amount or
  - Solve the issues and complete the collection or

- Take them to court and file a suit for collection of the said amount (In India NCLT and the consumer court are very good options).
- Simply write them off and forget about it.

3. Creditors

Your vendors are the ones who along with your bankers form the 2 pillars on which your business runs. Keeping them happy is of utmost importance and so is keeping honest with them. Since we are talking negative cash flows, the first tendency is to delay vendor payments. And to take them for granted.

Please never do that mistake. Instead, take them into confidence and be very transparent with them. You can do the following: -

- Tell them honestly your financial position and your plans for the turnaround.
- Try and get longer payment periods from existing vendors. Offer paying interest to them for the additional credit period if that helps.
- For existing overdues which you are not in a position to pay, negotiate for payment deferrals and payment plans (e.g. to be paid in 10 months with 10% p.a. interest) with critical suppliers.
- Settle with non-critical suppliers. (e.g. Settled for 75% of the outstanding amount payable over the next 6 months).
- With a few, simply stop paying them till you have the surplus cash flow.

This will help you kick start your production and also stretch that working capital the maximum.

You will, for sure, face problems with a few vendors who will create a lot of nuisance, you will have the face them and take it as it comes.

4. Lenders

Lenders form the next important part of your business. They have been supportive during your growth phase and would want you to really turn around your business. However, they have to work within the framework of regulations of the land and may help you only in limited ways. You should follow the following steps in your negotiations with your lender.

- *Take Banks and Financial Institutions in confidence and make them a part of your turnaround plan.*

  Trust will become the key factor which will decide whether the bank and its management will support you or not in the turnaround process. There are ways and means available with the bankers to support a client in times of need and to ensure that it does not gets tagged as a stressed account. But those doors are open to only clients that they have faith in.

By making the bankers a part of your turnaround plans and keeping them informed of everything that is happening is a good thing to do most of the times.

More often than not, they will give you solutions and also connect you to other people, turnaround specialists, Private Equity Players, and other businesses that can help. They are one of the best networked people on this planet, PERIOD.

- **Overcommunicate**

  With Bankers, you have to overcommunicate. Send them every little positive update that you have. Send them updates on how the turnaround plan is progressing. This will keep their trust levels up and also indicate bona-fide of the promoters and his efforts to revive the business. It will give you a fighting chance that the bankers will accept what you are requesting as they really love transparency.

- *Ask for New Limits and Negotiate longer repayment plans with your lenders.*

  As part of the restructuring plan, always ask for more money (you have to justify the need) and also for a longer repayment tenure for your existing debt. Newer limits will help with working capital and the longer repayment tenure will help with balancing the monthly cash flow by reducing debt servicing outflows.

  The Bankers here are governed by the rules of the land, but there are ways and means in which they can help while still staying within the framework. For example, they might not be able to offer a cash credit limit to you as working capital, but instead may be in a position to offer Bill Discounting Limits.

Banking rules and regulations have a lot of loopholes in terms of interpretation and understanding and bankers may help.

- **Delay any coercive action as long as possible.**

  In case there is real stress in business and you are defaulting on your payments, then the bankers have the right to take over your company (through NCLT in India), Repossess your assets which are mortgaged to them and to enforce personal and corporate guarantees.

  While they have the right, they are really not very inclined to exercise this as more often than not, they do not recover the full amount lent to you by going down this route.

  By keeping in touch with the bankers and giving them the confidence that your turnaround plan is working, you may be able to delay these actions.

  Please note that this is only to buy some time for your turnaround efforts to bear fruit. As soon as you are able, start paying them back. You have borrowed money and you are responsible for paying it back. Its ethical and moral thing to do.

5. **One Counter-Intuitive Thought: Save 10% from every receipt in a different account and do not spend it.**

   This was discussed earlier in the book. So, we will just leave it here and end it by saying that with 10% (or 5% if you are more comfortable with a lower percentile) kept away, you will still be in equal amount of monthly stress, just that now you will also have some money at the end of the day to take care of real emergencies.

6. **Assets**

   This is one part of the business which is often ignored. When business is stressed out, this is one place from where some quick funds can be generated. Let's see the 2 primary ways in which we can do this.

   - **Sell all non-core assets**

     Do you have an old machine lying which you do not use anymore? Sell it.

     Do you have an office? Can you shift the office to the factory? Sell the office.

     Do you have 3 trucks? Can you hire trucks from outside? Sell it.

     Do you have old computers, printers and furniture lying around in your office which are not in use? Sell it.

     Just walk around your business premises and I am sure you will find a ton of things which you do not use anymore. Sell it.

- **Liquidate all the excess inventory**

   As with your assets, look around your godown.

   Is there a lot of scrap lying around? Sell them.

   Is there a lot of finished goods which the customer had rejected? Sell them.

   Is there too much good inventory with you (You might have produced them in anticipation of an order which never came)? Offer them to the customer at a discounted price. If he does not want it, sell it in scrap.

   Is there some raw material which you have not used for 6 months or so? Sell them.

   Liquidate all excess inventory and free up your cash. Cash stuck in dead inventory is not earning you anything. The same cash deployed in moving products earn you 10-15% margin in each cycle. With 4 cycles, you will make 40%-50% profits on the amount so freed up from this excess inventory. Take the loss today and sell them. Generate that cash flow.

VI PRODUCTIVITY:

Productivity essentially indicates how well and efficiently you are using a resource available to you. There are three critical resources which every business has

1. People
2. Fixed Assets
3. Working Capital

Judicious use of the above 3 resources will ensure business success. Misuse of any of the 3 will definitely lead to sickness and ultimate demise of the business. Let's look at each one of them in a little more detail.

1. What are your sales per employee? Is it at least seven times the salary you pay?

The single most important parameter to measure your total wage bill to the revenues that your company generates. The higher this number, the better.

Let's look at them with a few live examples from large listed corporates: -

Company (2019 data)	Revenues	Wage Bill	Revenues / Wage Bill
	('000 Crs)		
Hindustan Unilever Ltd	38,224	1747	21.9
Tata Motors Limited	68,764	4273	16.1

What we are asking you to do is to initially touch the number of 7 times and then over a period of time improve it more than 10 times. Anything less than 7 times is really unsustainable.

2. **What is you Fixed Asset to Turnover Ratio?**

The second ratio measures the efficiency of asset utilization. It is simple formula where you divide your revenues with your fixed assets (Plant and Machinery + land and Building).

The bigger this number, the better it is. Normally, you should be able to do an annual turnover of over 4 times the value of your assets. The logic behind this being: -

Asset Value	100
Annual Revenue	400
Net profits	10%
Net Profits	40
Asset Payback period (asset value / Annual profits)	2.5 years

Essentially with this calculation, the investment should pay back for itself in 2.5 years. Even with a slightly lower profits or interest payment to purchase the asset, it should be able to payback for itself in 3 years.

This does not apply for utilities or infra assets where the payback period of 7-10 years is also acceptable (in some cases like power, even longer is acceptable).

3. Working Capital Turnover Ratio

This number tells us how well a company is generating its sales with respect to the working capital of the company. Working capital of a company is the difference between the current assets and current liabilities of a company.

The formula for calculating this ratio is by dividing the sales of the company by the working capital of the company.

Working Capital Turnover Ratio Formula = Sales/ Working Capital

Let's look at a couple working capital turnover ratio examples to bring some context as to why this metric is so useful for measuring efficiency.

Say Company A had net sales of 750,000 last year and working capital of 75,000. Company A's working capital turnover ratio is 10, which means the company spent that 75,000 ten times to generate its 750,000 in sales.

Company B, on the other hand had 750,000 in sales and 125,000 in working capital, resulting in a working capital turnover ratio of 6. Company B spent its working capital only six times throughout the year to generate the same level of sales as Company A.

As you may have guessed, a high ratio is better. The more sales you can bring in per unit of working capital deployed, the better off you are. It's generally considered a good thing to redeploy your working capital more times per year to gain your year's net sales figures, as it means that money is flowing easily in and out of your business and is working to make you more money.

In our example, Company A's working capital is doing exactly that — it's working for the company. It's working for the company ten times in a year, while Company B's working capital is only working six times. Yet both companies have generated the same amount of sales. It looks like Company A's money is being made to work harder than Company B's money is.

This metric is meant to help you compare the efficiency of your operations to your competitors or others in your sector, or to shed light on whether your operations are making progress year after year.

There can be very typical situation of negative working capital. It essentially means that the customer is paying you in advance and you pay your suppliers after some time. In this kind of a business, the company can expand very rapidly as technically, they do not need any money to sell.

If your business has to grow, you have to utilize your working capital very efficiently and ensure that you achieve a number of 8 or more. A working capital turnover ratio of less than 4 will be very difficult to sustain unless you have more than 25% profit margin on every transaction.

VII   MANAGEMENT AND CULTURE:

1. Doing the Right Thing

A business in the end is defined by its culture. TATAs are known for doing the right thing and sticking to its word. Whether it was recently paying off DOCOMO a Billion Dollars as per the agreed terms, even when they had a way out behind the rules of the country, or it was opening up Mumbai Taj Mahal for Doctors and Nurses fighting COVID 19. There are thousands of such stories of ethics and of doing the right thing.

Another story which I just read is below (a little long, but worth a read):

It was the year 1946. Germany stood devastated by the Second World War. The Allies had won the war, and many German cities, including Munich, had been severely damaged by the British Royal Air Force.

On one gloomy morning that year, at the Munich Railway station, stood the Directors of Krauss Maffei, the reputed German engineering Company. They were waiting for the arrival of their guests from India. Founded in 1838, Krauss Maffei was a leading maker of locomotives of various types, and an engineering company with a formidable reputation. Unfortunately, the Company now stood devastated by the World War, since their factories had been destroyed by the Allied Forces.

The guests from India got down from their train. If you had been there, you would have seen JRD Tata, the young, tall, lanky Chairman of the Group, get off the train. And accompanying him was a forty-year old engineer, Sumant Moolgaonkar, representing TELCO (now Tata Motors). They had come to Munich for discussions with Krauss Maffei, regarding the manufacture of locomotives in India. What they found, instead, were scenes of destruction and ruin.

The Germans requested the Indians to take some of their unemployed engineers to India, along with their families, and provide them jobs and shelter. The Directors of Krauss Maffei are reported to have told the Tata Directors – "They are very skilled people. They will do whatever you ask them if you take care of them. They can also teach your people."

This would have to be done without a formal contract, because the British, who were still ruling India, had forbidden Indian Companies from having any contracts with German Corporations, during those times of the World War.

The Tata Directors agreed to this request, and assured the Germans that their people would be well looked after. The German engineers from Krauss Maffei then came to India, and they were provided good jobs and housing by the Tata Group. They were well taken care of, and they also rendered great service to Tata Motors. In 1945, Tata Motors had signed an agreement with the Indian Railways for manufacture of steam locomotives, and this is where the German engineers provided valuable technical expertise. They helped the Company manufacture locomotives, which were amongst the Company's very first products.

In 1947, India became independent. In the 1950s, Tata Motors moved on to manufacture trucks in collaboration with Daimler Benz. Many years had now passed since that fateful meeting at the Munich Railway Station. Germany had substantially recovered from the ravages of the war, and the reconstruction effort had borne great fruit. In one of these happier years, the Board of Directors of Krauss Maffei was surprised to suddenly receive a letter from India.

This letter was from the Tata Group. It offered grateful thanks for the services of the German engineers, and it contained an offer of compensation to Krauss Maffei for the skills which had been transferred by the Germans to Tata Motors. Krauss Maffei was surprised, even taken aback at this offer. There was no legal contract, and therefore no obligation for the Tata Group to pay any compensation. In fact, I think, neither did this expectation exist, because the Tata Group had helped by providing jobs and shelter to the otherwise unemployed German engineers, during those dark days. So, the Germans were astonished, as they read the Tata letter.

This story was narrated many, many years later, in the 1970s, by Directors of Krauss Maffei, to Arun Maira, then a senior Director of Tata Motors.

One interesting and unexpected sidelight of this story occurred when Tata Motors was asked to provide a legally binding financial guarantee in the 1970s, but this was rendered very difficult because of the Indian Government's regulations at that time. This matter was taken up to German bankers, who said that a guarantee on a Tata letterhead, signed by the Chairman, was more valuable than any banker's guarantee.

I do not know what exact thoughts ran through the minds of Tata Directors in the 1950s before they sent that letter to Krauss Maffei, offering compensation where none was agreed upon or expected. But I think the Tata Group did this because it was the right thing to do.

The right thing to do is never defined by formal agreements or legal contracts alone. Neither is it defined by the expectations that others have of us. What is right is defined by our own high expectations of ourselves, by the culture of fairness and trust that we wish to establish. Are we being truly fair to the people and the Companies we work with? We always know, if we listen deeply enough to our inner voice, whether we are being totally fair and right. The Krauss Maffei story holds such a beautiful lesson for all of us.

2. Transparent and regular communication

It's tempting for business leaders to give every announcement or change within the company a positive spin, but this can actually do more harm than good. You can usually pick up on this type of PR-heavy strategy, and it's unlikely to foster feelings of trust in the company.

I would advise companies to "stop sugarcoating your communication. Include your employees in discussions about important business matters, and ask for their help in solving problems. They will rally around you, and this collaboration will strengthen your entire team."

If you value this kind of collaborative environment, look for signs of the regular communication such teamwork requires. Companies that believe in transparency will keep employees updated about what's going on in the organization through internal newsletters or other means.

Don't Delay Dispensing Information

Regular workplace surprises are an easy way to lose trust in an organization, but the fix is simple. Transparent companies stay on top of information and make sure employees are informed as soon as possible through official company announcements. They send an internal memo if there is a change in company policy or if they need to address a company-wide issue. Look for companies that seek to do this before word of changes trickles down to employees from other sources. This will prevent miscommunication and gossip.

3. Give Responsibility, Empower, Trust,

Finally, Trust Your people. Give them targets and then give them the tools to complete the task. Give them the right to make decisions and then get out of the way.

Not trusting your people and team to do the right thing also throws a light on your insecurities and petty thinking.

Your organization will never grow if you try to do everything yourself.

Give Responsibility. Empower Your Team and Then Get the Hell out of the way.

Epilogue/Conclusion

In the end, turnarounds are hard. Its blood, sweat, tears, bruises and deep cuts. Everyday is a new struggle to survive, another mountain to climb, another problem to solve, another burden to lift. And even after you give it your everything and then a little more, the business may still not survive.

All I can think of is the lyrics of an old Hindi Movie.

मैं जिंदगी का साथ निभाता चला गया
हर फ़िक्र को धुवें में उडाता चला गया

बरबादियों का शौक माना फिजुल था,
बरबादियों का जसन मनाता चला गया
मैं जिंदगी का साथ निभाता..

जो मिल गया उसी को मुक़दर समझ लिया,
जो खो गया मैं उसको भुलाता चला गया
मैं जिंदगी का साथ निभाता..

गम और ख़ुशी में फरक ना महसुस हो जहाँ
मैं दिल हो उस मुक़ाम में लाता चला गया

मैं जिंदगी का साथ निभाता चला गया
हर फ़िक्र को धुवें में उडाता चला गया..

Keep your head high. Keep working. Keep grinding. Give it your all. Even if you fail in the turnaround, don't let go of the lesson. Live to fight another day. Start another journey, start another business. Ensure that succeeds. Nothing can stop you but yourself. And You and Only You can make it happen.

About the Authors

Saurabh Maheshwari

The Author started his career in Sales with Bharat petroleum Corporation Limited selling Lubricants in 2003 and then switching to financial sector in 2004. He has worked with ICICI Bank and Reliance Capital, predominantly in the lending side of business and has handled large teams and geographies.

He currently has his own Boutique Investment Banking Firm since 2013. He also is involved in turning around a large restaurant chain in western India as its consulting CFO and made it profitable within a span of 15 months.

Over the last 17 years, He has studied and assessed financials of over 5000 small and medium sized corporates across industries and geographies and is involved in loans of over 5000 Crs.

His current startup is one in the finance space providing analytics to restaurants and helping them with data driven decision making.

He is an MBA from NMIMS, leading Business School in India and currently resides in Pune with his family.

His earlier book "Managing Your Finance during CRISIS" is available on Amazon Kindle and reached #18 on Amazon Bestsellers Rankings (India) and #2 in Amazon Bestseller Ranking (US).

You can read more about Saurabh at his businesses at

https://www.linkedin.com/in/saurabhprofile/

www.devmaheshwari.com

www.fnbanalytica.com.

Saurabh can be reached at sm@devmaheshwari.com

Ram Parthasarathy

Ram has about 40 years of rich experience in spearheading business operations with key focus on top-line growth and bottom-line profitability, while ensuring optimal cost and quality. Strong focus on lean manufacturing, internal efficiency, achievement of international quality systems, and aggressive business development. Extensive experience in turning around businesses, and returning struggling businesses to profitability through restructuring, resource optimization and efficiency management.

He is currently busy in turning around a company in the capital goods space.

Ram is an Alumnus of IIT Delhi (Batch of 1977) and then completed his executive education from IIM Ahmedabad. He is also a Certified iCEO by CEO Europe.

He currently resides in Pune with his family.

You can read more about Ram at

https://www.linkedin.com/in/ramparthasarathy/

Ram can be reached at rp_42@rocketmail.com

www.ingramcontent.com/pod-product-compliance
Lightning Source LLC
Chambersburg PA
CBHW030952240526
45463CB00016B/2524